Divorced
7 Keys to making it through your parents' divorce

Dedication

This book is dedicated to my parents, my brother, step-brother, and bonus dad. I love each of you!

1

Introduction

If you're reading this book, you might be dealing with your parents' separation or divorce. I went through it and made it out just fine and so can you. My parents divorced when I was six years old and my brother was two. I'm now ten and I wrote this book because I want to help other boys and girls. I came up with seven things that were really hard to deal with. I want to explain them and tell you how I handled them. Consider these ideas to help you through this challenging time. Write these ideas down somewhere in your room as reminders to help you and your parents through their divorce. I also have space for you to think about the ideas and write your thoughts here in the book. I hope this book helps you through this tough time. Remember, you'll be just fine.

Key #1:
Two homes

Once your parents split up, having two homes might not be easy. You may feel as if you got divorced, not just your parents. If you are like me, you love both of your parents. However, when your parents split up, you wanted them back together. But since that likely won't happen, you will now have two homes instead of one. Here are some tips if you want to spend time with each parent once they are separated.

What works for me is alternating weeks with each parent. One week I will stay with my mom and the next week I stay with my dad. This works for me because I love them both a lot and like spending a lot of time with each of them. It's not a perfect schedule and I still miss the other parent when I am not with them. How much time do you want to spend with your mom? How much time do you want to spend with your dad?

Fortunately, I have an iPad and I can call and text my parents whenever I want to talk to them. I also text them and they text me to see how I am doing. If you don't have your own device, try to set a time to talk each day so that you can stay in touch.

What days and times would be best to talk to dad when I am with mom?

_____

_____

_____

_____

_____

_____

_____

_____

_____

_____

_____

_____

_____

What days and times would be best to talk to mom when I am with dad?

_____

_____

_____

_____

_____

_____

_____

_____

_____

_____

_____

_____

Let's say your parents live halfway across the country from each other. This is what my stepbrother goes through. If you're like my stepbrother, you usually stay half the year with one parent and half with the other. Try to call your parents every day when you're away from them. If you have a lot of money to spend, maybe you can book a flight to your other parent's house. If you're afraid of airplanes, talk to your parents about moving close together and tell them about the stress you're having around going to each parent.

If it's hard to go back and forth, or not see one of your parents enough, try talking to your parents about who you want to live with more and how many days you want to stay there. Let them know you love them both, but you may want more time with one or the other. I hope they understand.

Another issue with two homes is rule differences. I know some people have parents that like different things and argue about those differences. That might be why they decided to get divorced. For example, my mom doesn't like a game that I like to play, but my dad doesn't mind that I play it. But sometimes my mom still lets me play that game for a bit. Thanks mom!

Here are the rules at dad's house:

_____

_____

_____

_____

_____

_____

_____

_____

_____

_____

_____

_____

Here are the rules at mom's house:

_____

_____

_____

_____

_____

_____

_____

_____

_____

_____

_____

When you go back to the other parent, you may get questions. When a parent says "did you play that game?" or "did you eat candy?" I respectfully tell them what's been said, eaten or played stays at the house where it happened. That way I stay out of it.

I hope you enjoyed this chapter and can use some of my ideas to help you in your parents' divorce.

Key #2:
Toys and friends

If you've been dealing with the divorce for a while then you will be able to relate to this situation. Let's say that it's your birthday and you just got a new toy at your dad's house. You love playing with it and you really want to take it to your mom's house. But, your dad says he doesn't want it to get lost, so you can't take it to your mom's house. What do you do? Should you tell your mom that you want to stay with your dad for a bit longer? But then you'll miss your mom.

Sometimes my parents allow me to take things back and forth. But then I forget them at one house or the other. I haven't found a good solution for this problem yet. It sucks. What do you think is a good solution?

Things that should stay at dad's house:

_____

_____

_____

_____

_____

_____

_____

_____

_____

_____

_____

_____

Things that should stay at mom's house:

Friends are a different situation. At my dad's house, I have many cousins and friends to play with because my dad's family lives nearby. When I go to my mom's house, I don't get to see those friends and cousins as much. I have a different set of friends that I play with when I am with my mom and stepdad. I have gained more friends by having a stepdad because he has many friends that have children my age. Again, it's not easy but you can get through these tough times.

Key #3:
Counseling

I thought I was the only one with divorced parents until my middle school counselor started a group for kids like me. Counseling is not only a place for grown-ups who are dealing with divorce, but also for kids, too! Counselors have all types of activities to help you stay calm when dealing with the divorce. These activities will help you and soon you won't care much about the divorce, but it takes time. What I like about counseling is that you get to talk about the divorce, and you may play games with your counselor. Sometimes they will have stuffed animals for you to hold while you talk about your emotions. An activity that I did with my counselor was to learn how to breathe in and out nice and slow.

You might be afraid to go and talk to a counselor, but just remember that it will really help you with the divorce. Also, while you're waiting in the lobby for your turn in the counseling room, there will be some toys to play with so you won't be bored. Now parents, if you're reading this book, make sure to take your child to counseling until you think your child is healed and ready to move on. I still go to counseling from time to time.

Things that I'd like to talk about:

_____

_____

_____

_____

_____

_____

_____

_____

_____

_____

_____

_____

Techniques to help me stay calm and happy (e.g. breathing techniques):

_____

_____

_____

_____

_____

_____

_____

_____

_____

_____

_____

_____

25

Key #4:
Gaining a new sibling from the divorce and remarriage

Always try to think on the bright side of any situation. If one of your parents starts a new relationship, you might get a stepbrother or stepsister like I did. You might not like him or her at first, but try to find out what they like to do and play together. After a while, you might become best friends like we did.

Try to find things to do that each of you enjoy. I like riding bikes with my stepbrother and going to the park together. Everyone is different, so they may not know how to ride a bike, but you can teach him or her. Teaching them things is a great way to start a good relationship with your stepbrother or stepsister. Take my advice and try not to argue with your siblings. If you keep meeting up with them and doing fun things together, I'm sure you will feel like real siblings soon.

Key #5:
Vacations

Everybody loves vacations. Who said you can't have double the fun? I say you can! I am about to show you another part of the positive side of divorce. Let's say your dad is going to Hawaii and you get to go with him. Hawaii is known for the Pearl Harbor attack, Polynesian culture and beautiful beaches. Let's say you have a good time in Hawaii. You chill, sip on juice boxes, and relax. While in Hawaii, you and your siblings also get to buy souvenirs. But then you have to head back home because the trip is over. Once you get home, your mom announces that you are going on vacation with her! You are really excited and can't wait for the next trip. This is an example of double vacations! If your mom is planning a trip and so is your dad, get ready for double vacations!

Key #6:
Your Future

Your future is an important thing, so never mess around with it. Always think about who you want to be and what you want to do with your life. One thing I am looking forward to is getting a car! Then I can travel back and forth between the two homes as much as I need to.

Let's say you just received your driver's license and you want to visit your dad because he is having a big party, but mom is busy and can't take you. If you have a car, she may allow you to go, but she might say, "take your brother, too!" You and your brother get in the car, head to your dad's house and have a blast.

Try to think about the future. You are growing up and will be able to make your own decisions soon. It won't always be this challenging. Hang in there!

What I want to be when I grow up:

_____

_____

_____

_____

_____

_____

_____

_____

_____

_____

_____

_____

What I want my future to look like:

_____

_____

_____

_____

_____

_____

_____

_____

_____

_____

_____

_____

Key #7:
Painful Tears

Divorce happens and it hurts. It's okay to cry because it is heartbreaking. But it's not your fault. There is nothing wrong with you and you did not cause the divorce. Saying these things might help you:

This happened in my life. It's okay to feel emotions.

I didn't cause it. I can't control my parents.

I can only control my behavior and my decisions.

Keep saying these things every night to help you deal with the divorce and help yourself move on. My mom told me that some people can't work or even graduate because of their mulling over their parents' divorce. I made this book because I do not want you to fail in school, not go to college, or can't move on with your life. I hope you enjoyed this book and I hope it helps you. Good luck!

www.ingramcontent.com/pod-product-compliance
Lightning Source LLC
Chambersburg PA
CBHW080856120626
46553CB00009B/2657